IMAGES
of Rail

CENTRAL WYOMING
RAILROADS

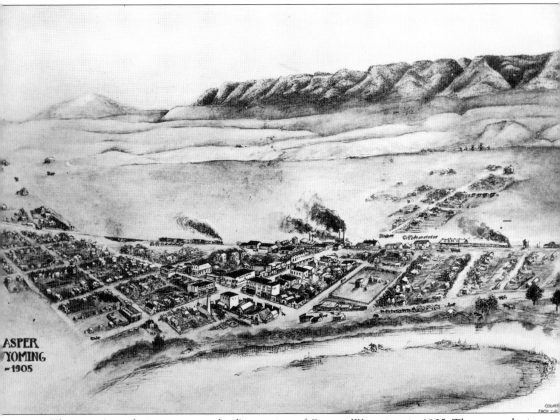

ASPER
YOMING
~1905

This artist's rendering portrays a bird's-eye view of Casper, Wyoming, in 1905. The scene depicts trains on the Chicago & North Western line, along with prominent early businesses including the Webel Mercantile Company, Richards and Cunningham Mercantile, and the Natrona Hotel. The Chicago, Burlington & Quincy line would not reach Casper until 1913. (Walter Jones Collection, Casper College Western History Center.)

ON THE COVER: On May 8, 1950, Pres. Harry S. Truman arrived in Casper aboard the presidential railcar *Ferdinand Magellan* on a visit to the Kortes Dam project west of town. Prior to getting off the train, he made a speech from the rear platform of the car to the waiting crowd of citizens and reporters. (Chuck Morrison Collection, Casper College Western History Center.)

IMAGES
of Rail

CENTRAL WYOMING RAILROADS

Con Trumbull

ARCADIA
PUBLISHING

Published by Arcadia Publishing
Charleston, South Carolina

Printed in the United States of America

Library of Congress Control Number: 2021937312

For all general information, please contact Arcadia Publishing:
Telephone 843-853-2070
Fax 843-853-0044
E-mail sales@arcadiapublishing.com
For customer service and orders:
Toll-Free 1-888-313-2665

Visit us on the Internet at www.arcadiapublishing.com

*This book is dedicated to the men and women of the rails and to the
memory of Linda Aston (January 22, 1943–September 12, 2020).*

CONTENTS

ACKNOWLEDGMENTS

First and foremost, I would like to thank my family and friends for their support not only for this project but for my many historical pursuits.

Thanks also go out to Rick Young, Michelle Bahe, and Anne Holman at the Fort Caspar Museum and Vince Crolla and Johanna Wickman at the Casper College Western History Center for providing many of the images in this book. They were instrumental in scanning images and providing much of the information. I also would like to send my thanks to Susan Bishop and the Cadoma Foundation and to the McCleary family for their images and information. Many members of the community helped identify features in the photographs and provided anecdotal stories for the captions, including Jared Kelly with insights of the railroads today and how they relate to historic features. A special thank-you goes out to Charles Eckerson. His knowledge gained from a lifetime love of trains and a 42-year railroad career, along with his openness to share images, stories, and quite a few laughs, brought everything together.

Finally, I would like to thank everyone at Arcadia Publishing who were unbelievably understanding and supportive through such an unusual year.

Credit for photographs from the Casper College Western History Center are abbreviated as CCWHC and the Wyoming State Archives, Department of State Parks and Cultural Resources, as Wyoming State Archives. Photographs from individual contributors are credited with the individual, organization, or family name.

All author royalties from the sale of this book benefit the Fort Caspar Museum Association, a nonprofit organization founded in 1987 to support the preservation and education activities at Fort Caspar Museum through financial support and volunteer time.

INTRODUCTION

The windswept plains of central Wyoming have long been a transportation corridor, beginning with Native American tribes who hunted up and down the North Platte River finding plentiful fish and game. Westward migration from the Eastern states began in earnest in the 1840s along the emigrant trails with long wagon trains passing through. The Pony Express, transcontinental telegraph, and stagecoach lines would all eventually follow these pioneering trails. It would not be until the 1880s when settlements would be firmly established along these same trail corridors.

Though settlements were founded, it would take the arrival of the railroads providing reliable transportation of goods, supplies, and people to make the settlements permanent. Construction of the early railroads was a complicated matter. Routes had to be surveyed and plotted for the graders to smooth out a roadbed. Cuts would be made through hills, and depressions filled with the earth from the cuts. Bridges had to be constructed and tunnels dug. Tracklaying started with wooden ties being laid out followed by two metal tie plates for the rails to lay on. Sections of rail were then placed down and the gauge, the distance between the rails, was checked before spikes were driven into the ties holding the rail in place. All this was done by hand by large construction crews organized like a small army.

As complicated as matters were for the construction itself, the business and financial side of the business was worse. Railroad companies had a myriad of subsidiaries, contractors, and subcontractors involved, creating a phone book of acronyms that most people would rather not have to muddle through. As such, the construction of the central Wyoming railroads will be referred to by the parent company that built the line or its primary subsidiary to create a simplified explanation for this work. There are numerous other references that explain these complex details for those who are interested.

Steam locomotives will be identified by the Whyte system of notation. For example, the locomotive on page 12 is a 4-4-0, which means there are four pilot wheels, four driving wheels, and no trailing wheels. Steam locomotives were designed for the work they were expected to perform. Passenger locomotives typically had tall driving wheels for speed, while freight locomotives had short drivers for power. Switch locomotives, being fairly small in comparison to main line engines, typically had no pilot or trailing wheels, which placed all of the locomotive's weight on the driving wheels, thus providing the traction needed to move strings of cars through railyards and industries.

This work covers the story of the two main railroads in the region, the Chicago & North Western, abbreviated as C&NW, and the Chicago, Burlington & Quincy, abbreviated as CB&Q. Additionally, the Fremont, Elkhorn & Missouri Valley will be abbreviated as FE&MV.

The first line into central Wyoming was built under the direction of the C&NW. Organizationally, things were complicated from the start. Two companies were incorporated for the construction of this line, the Wyoming Central to act as the construction company, and the FE&MV to operate the line. Trackage reached Orin and Douglas in 1886, followed by Glenrock in 1887 and Casper in

1888. A new construction company subsidiary, the Wyoming & Northwestern, was organized 10 years later to continue construction west, although actual construction did not begin until 1905.

Tracks made their way to Shoshoni, Riverton, and Lander in 1906. Plans had been made to extend the line over South Pass and eventually to the Pacific Ocean, but these plans were dropped when the C&NW negotiated a deal with the Union Pacific, and Lander became the westernmost terminus of the C&NW.

The CB&Q, also referred to as the Burlington in many texts, would reach Casper from the opposite direction. Track was laid into the town of Thermopolis in 1910, and soon after, construction began through the imposing Wind River Canyon. Despite construction and engineering challenges including the boring of multiple tunnels, the line was completed through to Boysen the next year. Grading of the line beyond this point was commenced, but the track was not laid until 1913, with the rails reaching Casper late that year. The next year, the line would progress to the connection with the Colorado & Southern at Orin Junction.

By the time the CB&Q had reached Casper, the development of the oil industry that would come to define the city was already well under way. Along with the growth due to the refineries, the city became a center for agriculture, industry, commercial companies, and social functions. While Lander was the western terminus of the C&NW, the line from that point to Casper was treated as little more than a branch line, with track conditions becoming so bad that a section had to be abandoned and a deal made with the CB&Q for trains to reach Shoshoni.

The rail connection to the rest of the world would bring immigrants from around the globe to the region, along with visits by presidents, royalty, and celebrities. Workers for the Civilian Conservation Corps came in on special trains during the Great Depression to complete public works projects, and World War II troop trains brought Army airmen for training at the Casper Army Air Base.

Freight trains hauled everything imaginable into the communities along the line, promoting construction and expansion and bringing modern conveniences to rural Wyoming. Oil products were shipped from Casper to points all over the country and for export overseas. Wool became an important product from ranches, and long livestock trains hauled animals to market.

The late 1950s through the 1960s saw the importance of the railroads steadily diminish. Automobiles, trucks, and airlines became the primary modes of transportation and shipping of local goods, leaving railroads to shift their operational focus. Once there were dozens of miles of track serving industries in the towns along the way, but these tracks were paved over or torn up. The switch to diesel locomotives removed the need for the large maintenance facilities for the steam locomotives. The job losses resulting from the closure of these facilities further diminished the railroads' importance to the local communities.

The C&NW ended service to the town of Lander in 1972. In 1995, the line was absorbed by the Union Pacific, and the tracks through Casper were abandoned the next year. The CB&Q went through several mergers, becoming the Burlington Northern, then the Burlington Northern Santa Fe, before becoming the BNSF Railway.

Today, BNSF trains still roll through Central Wyoming, though few individuals take notice and fewer still remember a time when the railroad was at the center of nearly every aspect of life. This book, while not intending to be a comprehensive history, strives to create a portrait of railroading in central Wyoming, and it is hoped that readers will get a sense of the lasting impacts to the region from these pioneering rails.

One

ARRIVAL OF THE RAILS

Workers lay track for the FE&MV during construction through central Wyoming around 1887. Surveyors would first map out the route, followed by the graders, who would prepare the roadbed. Track gangs laid the ties and rail so the gauge of the rails could be checked, then the spikes were driven into the ties and rock ballast placed so that trains could start to utilize the track. (Cutshaw Collection, CCWHC.)

Prior to the arrival of the railroad, travel across the plains of central Wyoming consisted of long, dusty days on a wagon slowly moving along dirt trails. While most people picture the classic covered wagon of Oregon Trail fame, by the end of the 1800s, the most popular choice was a simple farm wagon to haul goods. In addition to these, buckboards and stagecoaches transported people, mail, and express parcels up and down the Platte River valley. These pioneering trails would be followed by steel rails due to the gentle grades of the valley. (Above, David Historical Collection, CCWHC; below, Chuck Morrison Collection, CCWHC.)

Casper, Wyo., 1898.

The arrival of the railroad brought with it the ability to cheaply and efficiently ship goods into the region. Once these goods arrived in Casper, they would be distributed to the various businesses and industries that quickly opened. Part of the shipments would be picked up by freighters with long string teams who would transport goods to towns and ranches not directly connected to the rails. The discovery of oil in the Salt Creek Field would see 26-horse string teams transporting materials and heavy equipment to the field and barrels of oil back to Casper for processing and eventual shipment across the country by rail. This 1898 view was captured near what are now Elm and Midwest Streets. (Frances Seely Webb Collection, CCWHC.)

As railroad construction moved east from Glenrock in early 1888, the townsite of Casper began preparations for the railroad's arrival. After negotiating with ranches, the FE&MV constructed a depot on what was then the CY Ranch. The first passenger train arrived in Casper on June 15, 1888, pulled by a 4-4-0 American-type locomotive, spurring rapid development and incorporation as a town in April 1889. (Kukura True Collection, CCWHC.)

A group has gathered on the platform of the first FE&MV Depot in Casper in 1909. This building quickly became a social center to the small town, providing a solid connection to the outside world. To the left, a wooden C&NW boxcar sits at a freight barn. (Wyoming State Archives.)

Standing in his office at the C&NW Depot in 1913 is William F. Dunn, the first station agent for that railroad in Casper. A station agent was tasked with selling tickets, checking baggage, and billing freight. An important part of any railroad operation, the job has always involved vast amounts of paperwork to ensure that proper fares were collected, freight bills were made up correctly, and all required reports were filed. Many of the records created in such offices were maintained for decades and have provided invaluable insights into the development of railroads and the West. Locally, the railroad allowed citizens in central Wyoming to access reliable freight transportation for goods as well as fast, safe travel along the Platte River valley and to the rest of the country. Industry and warehouses that sprang up along the tracks brought increased need for freight traffic, and additional workers were quickly hired to assist Dunn. (Fort Caspar Museum.)

One of three photographs of the Burlington yards under construction around 1914, this view captures a spreader on a work train. This contraption, in the center of the image, has winged blades that can reshape the ballast along the rails, providing structure and proper drainage for the track. During the winter, this device could also push snow away from the tracks. Behind the spreader is the water tower that fed water to the shop buildings and to water columns in the yard to replenish steam locomotive tenders. In the upper right is the roundhouse building nearing completion. (Frances Seely Webb Collection, CCWHC.)

Just to the right of the roundhouse is an A-frame of the turntable. Turntables were vital parts of railyards in the days of steam that turned the locomotive for its next assignment. Additional work cars for the construction trains stand on the tracks. (Frances Seely Webb Collection, CCWHC.)

The tracks stretch east out of Casper to the connection at Orin near Douglas. In a few short years, the area around the yard would boom into the industrial and commercial center of Casper. These photographs were taken by the Wiswall Studio of Denver for the Casper Townsite Company around 1914. The proposed depot site was just to the right. (Frances Seely Webb Collection, CCWHC.)

While the arrival of the first passenger train into a town was cause for elaborate celebrations, construction trains were actually the first to reach the community. In this photograph, the crew of C&NW No. 1210, a 4-6-0 ten-wheeler, poses with their engine and the construction crew in October 1906. It makes up an unassuming consist for the first train into the town of Lander. In addition to carrying the supplies needed for the physical construction of the tracks, these trains contained bunk, kitchen, and dining cars for the workers as well as mobile shops and offices to keep the construction process running smoothly. The ties, tie plates, spikes, and rails were all carried along on the train and were laid by hundreds of workers, mostly by hand. Once construction was completed, plans could be made by town leaders and the railroad for proper celebrations to open the line. (Cutshaw Collection, CCWHC.)

The first C&NW passenger train from Casper to Lander in 1906 seemed to bring out the entire population of the small communities along the way. Passengers on the train included many of central Wyoming's prominent businessmen and their families, who celebrated the new connection to the world and the promise of economic growth that it brought. The train traveled from Casper to the end of the line at Lander, which soon became known as the town "where the rails end and the trails begin." As one of the largest communities along the route, the citizens of Shoshoni turned out in force to celebrate the arrival of the train on its return trip to Casper. Here, passengers and residents pose in their finest clothes for a commemorative photograph shortly before the train departs town. (Thompson/Bryant Collection, CCWHC.)

Pictured around 1895, a C&NW train leaves Casper heading east toward Glenrock. At this point, the settlement of Casper amounted to little more than a cow town. By connecting the town to the rest of the country, its importance to central Wyoming would grow exponentially, and the population was set to explode. Construction materials, furnishings, and other goods arriving by train led to the construction of larger buildings and the growth of industry. Connecting agricultural producers to larger markets allowed ranches to expand their operations, while irrigation projects, partially sponsored by the railroads, led to the growth of farms. With the development of the nearby Salt Creek Oil Field and the opening of Casper's first refinery this same year, the railroad was well in place to meet the demands of this growing industry. (Sheffner-McFadden Collection, CCWHC.)

Two

SERVING CASPER

The primary purpose of a railroad company was to provide transportation services, but these companies also aspired to become pillars of the communities they served. Harry Evans (right), seen in his office on the second floor of the depot, was appointed by the CB&Q as special representative of the railroad. He attended community meetings and presented funds to a variety of local groups and projects. (Casper Star-Tribune Collection, CCWHC.)

CHICAGO, BURLINGTON & QUINCY R. R. DEPOT.

Reaching Casper in 1913, the CB&Q built a temporary depot for operations. After two years, construction of a permanent depot began in May 1915. The building was completed on February 3, 1916, for a cost of $85,000. It was most often referred to as the Burlington Depot and has remained in continuous service ever since. This postcard image dates from the 1920s. (Fort Caspar Museum.)

BURLINGTON DEPOT, CASPER WYO. © WAS. # 27

Shown soon after construction was completed, a passenger train has just arrived at the Burlington Depot. A Railway Post Office car is directly to the right of the building, followed by coaches. The truck in the center of the photograph belonged to the Wyoming Transfer, Moving, and Storage Company and was used to transfer baggage and packages from the depot to their final destination. (Fort Caspar Museum.)

CHICAGO & NORTHWESTERN DEPOT AND THE MONUMENT.

Located near the center of Casper, the C&NW Depot strove to lead the town into the modern era. Though surrounding the depot were simple dirt streets, the installation of concrete sidewalks, electric street lamps, and a park with the Pioneer Monument in the center created a space that sought to portray a well-developed city. (Fort Caspar Museum.)

When it was built, the C&NW Depot in Casper was considered the finest to be found on that line west of Omaha. The building boasted steam heat, electric lights, and tile floors, and was thoroughly modern in every respect. The style of the building followed a classic depot design that could be found in towns all over the United States and included a bay window for the station master. This image was captured in the 1920s. (Fort Caspar Museum.)

This photograph looking southwest across Center Street was taken in 1914. A passenger train has arrived at the C&NW Depot, out of frame to the right. Buckboards and automobiles share the dirt street. Note the railroad crossing sign advising people to "Look Out for the Cars." Behind the passenger train, boxcars have been spotted next to the freight barns. (Frances Seely Webb Collection, CCWHC.)

Thomas Carrigen, a famous Casper photographer, captured this rare view of the C&NW Depot looking to the southwest on October 3, 1941. The waiting rooms were on the left side of the building, company offices upstairs, and baggage and express rooms on the right side. The Pioneer Monument is on the left. (Wyoming State Archives.)

This image, taken from the roof of a boxcar, shows a train passing the C&NW Depot. On the far left, a caboose awaits its next assignment. These cars were once commonplace at the rear of freight trains, providing space for the conductor to do his reports as well as seats in the cupola for the brakemen to inspect the train for any problems. (Thompson Collection, CCWHC.)

C&NW No. 2130 is crossing Wolcott Street on October 17, 1928. Behind the locomotive is a warehouse for the Richards and Cunningham Company, an early dry goods store. The locomotive is an 0-6-0 switch locomotive, used to switch freight cars into and out of the industries along the track and make up the freight trains to be pulled behind larger main line locomotives. (Wyoming State Archives.)

Chicago & North Western Depot,
Casper, Wyoming.

Made for
The Casper Townsite Co.

Photo by
Wiswall,
Denver.

In this c. 1912 scene, a passenger train has arrived at the C&NW Depot led by No. 10, a 4-6-0 ten-wheeler. "Train time" at any depot was always a busy affair. In addition to passengers arriving or leaving, baggage, mail, and express shipments would have to be transferred. Overseeing all of this, the conductor would ensure the train was ready to depart on time. (Francis Seely Webb Collection, CCWHC.)

A VISIT TO THE MIDWEST REFINERY
WYOMING OIL MENS CONVENTION
CASPER WYO. MAY 28 29 1912

Photo by
The Gleason
Studio,

Recognizing the role that oil would play in the state, Gov. Bryant B. Brooks called for an oil convention in 1910. Two years later, the Wyoming Oil Men's Convention was held in Casper in May 1912, and attendees visited the Midwest Refinery for a tour. Behind the crowd, Union Tank Line tank cars are spotted on a track for loading. (McCleary family.)

The CB&Q Depot was no longer the gateway to Casper that it had once been when this photograph was taken around 1962. As people turned away from passenger trains as a primary method of travel, the importance of such depots waned. Though passenger service ended in 1967, freight traffic continued, and the depot would still serve the railroad, housing company offices. (Sheffner-Butler-Schultz Collection, CCWHC.)

Shipping freight required that the appropriate paperwork be completed to ensure proper billing and tracking of the shipment. Here, office workers process paperwork in the CB&Q freight office on the first floor of the depot in 1916. The identified workers are May Royal (second from left), Genevieve Sheffner (third from left), and Henry Simmons, the boss (far right). (Sheffner-Butler-Schultz Collection, CCWHC.)

In 1932, Center Street still crossed the west end of the CB&Q yards. Very little of this scene except for the depot building is recognizable today. A passenger train has stopped at the depot, while a switch engine with brakemen riding the footboards is at the edge of the crossing. The tower is for the watchman, who would have to manually lower the crossing gates to stop automobile traffic. To the left, the large water tanks stand with the shop facilities behind them. Looking closely at the photograph, workers can be seen all over the yard, and a steam-powered crane can be found stored next to the icehouse in the center of the image. The white building to the left of the brick depot was the original depot building, and the freight house is between the two. Today, there are few remnants of the shop facilities, and Center Street is now an underpass at this location, eliminating a railroad crossing on one of Casper's main streets. (Wyoming State Archives.)

The use of the Burlington Depot would continually evolve as the focus of railroad operations changed. These rare images show the interior of the building in the late 1960s and were taken by Charles Eckerson, an employee of the railroad. Above, Jerry Storeim is in the ticket office. Passengers would purchase tickets through the window to the right, and on the counter is a ticket stamp. Below, Bob Miller, a machinist in the shop, paused for this photograph in the yard office. While the exterior of the building has essentially remained the same, the interior was extensively remodeled to better suit modern railroad operations. (Both, Charles Eckerson.)

At left, a tourist poses before boarding the train on August 4, 1942. Below, CB&Q diesel locomotive E7 unit No. 9926-A stands at the Burlington Depot with a short string of passenger cars. A far cry from the long passenger trains of the early 1900s, this train consists of a Railway Post Office, a coach, and a baggage car at the end. The train crew pauses for this 1960s photograph. From left to right are superintendent Jim Bowman, engineer Vern Trout, unidentified conductor and brakeman, a Mr. Murphy; trainmaster Ed Wagers, and unidentified fireman climbing into the cab. The smokestack behind the train was for the CB&Q powerhouse, torn down in May 1961. (Left, author's collection; below, Chuck Morrison Collection, CCWHC.)

The Burlington passenger train served more than just everyday travelers into and out of Casper. On this occasion, the regular train was dubbed the "Mustang Victory Special" and was used to take one of the Natrona County High School sports teams to a meet. At right, the cheerleaders take over the locomotive, while below, they take a moment to pose with the Pullman porter before boarding the train. (Both, Chuck Morrison Collection, CCWHC.)

The Railway Post Office was once central to the handling of the US mail. Sacks would be delivered to the car while it was standing at the station or hung from a special pole beside the tracks for the clerks to catch using a hook on the side of the car. Clerks would then sort the mail while the train was underway, preparing it for the next point along the line. The mail contract was often the most lucrative part of a passenger train, and the loss of these contracts spelled the end of many scheduled trains when trucks and airplanes took over. A postal car is being loaded at the Burlington depot in the above photograph, while below, the same car waits on a siding. Both photographs were taken in the 1960s. (Both, Charles Eckerson.)

All is quiet at the Burlington Depot in the 1960s image above looking to the east. Some of the depot's 14 baggage carts stand along the platform waiting to transfer baggage and express shipments from the train to the depot, and various passenger cars rest between assignments. Mail was still shipped on the train, though it was no longer sorted under way, so the Railway Post Office car has been removed from the consist. Soon after this photograph was taken, passenger service in Casper would be a thing of the past. The end for train No. 29 came in 1967, bringing with it the end of an era. Below is the last engine crew swap for the train in Casper. (Above, Chuck Morrison Collection, CCWHC; below, Charles Eckerson.)

The CB&Q passenger conductors and brakemen assigned to train No. 29 were highly proud of the service they provided. The conductor has become one of the most iconic figures in American railroading. Well dressed in the traditional suit and hat, the conductor was in charge of the train. Interacting with passengers, the shout of "all aboard," and the punching of the tickets only hinted at his duties. Train No. 29's end in 1967 saw conductor Arneson, pictured here, being the last conductor on the train into Casper. (Charles Eckerson.)

The end of passenger service through Casper came on September 2, 1967, with the last run of train No. 29. Though it would mark the end of nearly 80 years of passenger trains to central Wyoming, the last train boarded and left with no ceremony to mark its passing. The last passenger, above, stepped aboard the train, and conductor Wechworth prepared for departure. In the last few minutes before the train left, railroad employee Charles Eckerson chalked a farewell message on the buffer plate on the end of the train reading, "The End 9-2-67, good bye forever 29." (Both, Charles Eckerson.)

Large quantities of snow from the infamous blizzard of 1949, combined with the ever-present Casper winds, made for miserable conditions. Here, a view of the crossing near the C&NW Depot shows the blowing and drifting snow competing with a steam locomotive working to keep trains rolling. The crossing signals were referred to as "wig-wags" due to their swinging motion when activated. (Both, Chuck Morrison Collection, CCWHC.)

Considered one of the worst blizzards ever in the region, the blizzard of 1949 started on January 2, with additional storms and strong winds throughout the next two months bringing transportation to a standstill. Trains became stranded in the deep snows until rescue crews could reach them. After stalling in drifts, the snow threatened to completely bury these locomotives. (Fort Caspar Museum.)

In an effort to clear the tracks, a rotary snowplow was put to work cutting through drifts roughly 15 feet deep. Rotary plows have large rotating blades to cut through the snow and throw it off the right-of-way. While the rotary has a boiler to make steam to turn the blades, it is not self-propelled, so a locomotive is placed behind it. (Sheffner-McFadden Collection, CCWHC.)

With ground transportation all but impossible, the Army was called in to drop supplies to stranded trains, small towns, and ranches as well as hay to livestock and wildlife. Here, a C-46 drops supplies to a stranded train near Egbert. Crew members from a locomotive completely covered with snow are attempting to retrieve these packages before they are buried under the drifts. (Fort Caspar Museum.)

Among the most useful pieces of equipment in the maintenance fleets of the railroads were cranes that could be used in many aspects of operations. Above is a steam-powered Link-Belt crane, No. 224, that has a special bucket for cement hanging from the hook being used in an early construction project. Underneath the crane are gears that make it self-propelled. Below, CB&Q wrecking crane No. 204361 is hard at work cleaning up a derailment west of Casper. These cranes would be accompanied to the work site by a train carrying the wrecking crew, often providing bunk and kitchen space as well as hauling the blocking and rigging needed to complete the job. (Above, Thompson Collection, CCWHC; below, Charles Eckerson.)

Finding wide-open range with ample grass, many early central Wyoming ranches got their start in the wool industry. Wool sheared from the sheep would be packed into large sacks weighing around 1,000 pounds at the ranches and brought by string teams to the wool warehouses along the tracks. In the photograph above, wagons loaded with wool from the Banner Ranch southeast of Casper are seen near present-day Hat Six Road. Below, wagons, including a sheep wagon, from other ranches have arrived at the wool warehouses, where the sacks will be sorted and loaded into boxcars to be shipped to market. (Above, McCleary family, below Frances Seely Webb Collection, CCWHC.)

In the 1930s, Banner Ranch wool, above, has arrived at the wool warehouses by truck. The wool industry remained strong until the end of World War II in 1945, when the market crashed due to the sudden loss of demand. Many ranches in the area then made the decision to switch their operation from sheep to cattle. Though many sheep ranches remain, this was a fundamental shift in the agricultural character of central Wyoming that has lasted to the present day. Below, car No. 211239, called a drover's car, was placed at the end of livestock trains to provide bunk space for ranch hands traveling with the livestock to the stockyard. Seen in the Casper yard in 1963, the car has been placed in maintenance-of-way service to house track crews. (Above, McCleary family; below, author's collection.)

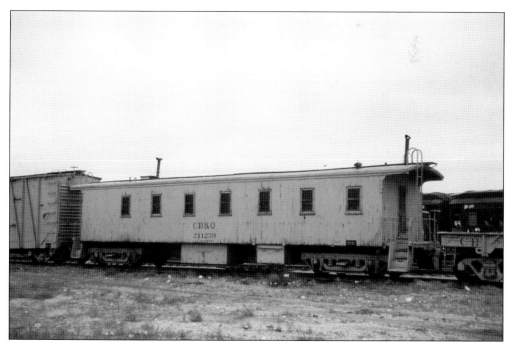

Steam locomotives were labor-intensive machines, often requiring hours of maintenance between assignments. This work was accomplished in the roundhouse, named for the curved shape of the building around a turntable. Attached to the building is shop space on the left. In addition to the mechanics at such facilities, workers called hostlers were in charge of preparing the locomotives for their next trip. The service area would also have facilities to load fuel and water into the tender. Coal-burning locomotives required that the ash pan be cleaned out, so an ash pit would typically be found. Service facilities would be small cities in themselves, complete with their own fire department, first aid team, and fraternal organizations. Many railroaders who started in the early 1900s began as apprentices, helpers, and callers. (Thompson Collection, CCWHC.)

To the left of the smaller tank in the photograph above is the A-frame of the turntable at the Burlington shops across from the depot. Unlike many styles of diesel locomotive, which can be operated equally well in forward or reverse, steam locomotives had to be turned to face the direction of travel. The turntable, a platform of track that could rotate in a full circle, was an expensive but elegant solution to this problem. Without such a device, a wye (tracks set up in the form of a three-point turn) or balloon loop would have to be employed, both of which required a lot of real estate and were time consuming to use. Below, this view of the back side of the roundhouse shows the end of the stationary steam boiler cutting through the wall. This boiler provided steam heat for the building and ran certain shop machines. (Both, Thompson Collection, CCWHC.)

C&NW shop workers pause from their duties for a group photograph on July 1, 1935. Railroad shop crews were composed of workers who possessed a wide range of skills, with each position handling a certain aspect of steam locomotive maintenance. Such positions included boilermakers, machinists, pipe fitters, welders, blacksmiths, painters, and their apprentices. (Wyoming State Archives.)

It was a quiet day in the C&NW roundhouse when Casper photographer Thomas Carrigen snapped these images of the interior on October 2, 1933. Locomotive No. 1484 is spotted under the smoke jack, a metal chimney that allows for smoke from a hot locomotive to exit the building. Various parts and tools can be seen lining the wall of the shop. (Wyoming State Archives.)

One of the primary functions of the roundhouse was to get the steam locomotives ready for their assignments. Hostlers were responsible for building a fire, cleaning the ash pans, greasing, oiling, adding water treatment chemicals, and ensuring the locomotive tender was loaded with fuel and water. Typically, once a fire was lit, the locomotive would remain hot around the clock unless the fire needed to be dropped to make repairs or if there was a boiler wash or inspection scheduled. In addition, light repairs would be made to the locomotive ranging from fixing a leaking valve to repairs of spring rigging in the running gear. Heavier repairs required locomotives to be sent to a heavy repair facility elsewhere on the railroad. (Both, Wyoming State Archives.)

In this view of the early days of the Burlington yard, temporary offices still on wheels but with telegraph lines attached are seen on the right. In the center is a caboose, and to the left, a handcar is sitting in the dirt. An old boxcar with wheels removed serves as a shed until more permanent structures can be built. (Thompson Collection, CCWHC.)

The importance of the roundhouses in Casper had been greatly diminished by the time this photograph was taken of the C&NW roundhouse in the 1960s. Today, nothing remains of either the CB&Q or the C&NW roundhouse and steam servicing facilities. This same fate awaited similar facilities all over the country. (Fred Thomason Collection, CCWHC.)

CB&Q locomotive No. 5127, a 2-8-2 Baldwin built in 1922, had the distinction of being the last steam locomotive to pull a regular train out of Casper. This last trip occurred on December 16, 1953, with engineer Ludwig and fireman Marsh in the cab. This trip ended over 65 years of steam locomotives operating in central Wyoming. The locomotive above was scrapped less than two years later and was photographed at an unknown location. The end of passenger service also saw the end of streamlined diesel units through Casper. The last of these is seen below on September 2, 1967. (Above, author's collection; below, Charles Eckerson.)

The Brotherhood of Locomotive Engineers and Trainmen (BLE) is the oldest labor union in the United States, tracing its roots back to the Brotherhood of the Footboard, which was organized by engineers of the Michigan Central Railroad in 1863. The union tried first and foremost to engage in open negotiations with the railroad companies. However, when railroads refused to engage or if what the union felt were reasonable demands were not met, workers would go on strike. Below, members of BLE Local 184 (from left to right) Eric Kreigh, Bill Garner, and Harvey Stoneking are on strike outside of the Burlington Depot in the early 1980s. (Both, Casper Star-Tribune Collection, CCWHC.)

Use of the railroads by local industries steadily decreased from the 1950s. Tracks that once snaked through yards, refineries, and industrial zones were slowly pulled up, covered in pavement, or simply forgotten. Today, not much is left, but there are still remnants of these tracks that can be found. Here, C&NW No. 4506 traverses some very rough industrial track on September 25, 1982. (Casper Star-Tribune Collection, CCWHC.)

Appearing to be in the dead of winter, this C&NW diesel has arrived in Casper after battling through blowing snow and drifts. The date was May 1, 1967, and record low temperatures combined with heavy snowfall covered much of central and northeastern Wyoming. A reporter felt that the snow on the train "sculpted a picture of Santa Claus" and brought a touch of Christmas to the air. (Casper Star-Tribune Collection, CCWHC.)

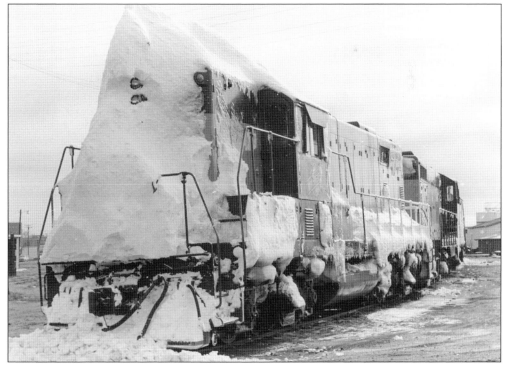

Business in Casper, while less than that of the boom years for the railroad, maintained sufficient traffic to justify the C&NW line when this photograph was taken on July 14, 1988. In October 1995, the C&NW merged with the Union Pacific Railroad, which abandoned the Casper line in 1996. The rails may have been torn up, but the railroad left a lasting impact on the community. The strip of land through town where the main line once ran has been preserved and repurposed as a popular bike trail. Those driving to Glenrock on the Old Glenrock Highway can still see the grade of the right-of-way along with numerous bridges and culverts. (Casper Star-Tribune Collection, CCWHC.)

Three

ACCIDENTS ON THE RAILS

Casper has the unfortunate distinction of playing host to the worst railroad disaster in the history of the state of Wyoming after heavy rains hit the area on September 27, 1923. CB&Q train No. 30, the overnight train to Denver, left Casper unaware that the bridge over Cole Creek had washed out due to the flooded stream, resulting in the locomotive and five passenger cars piling up. (CCWHC.)

At 8:30 p.m., the train departed the CB&Q depot after the engineer had been informed that the bridge was in sound condition, but he was also instructed to use extreme caution along the entire line. Unbeknownst to anyone, the heavy rainfall caused Cole Creek to overflow its banks. The bridge, not built to withstand such an event, washed out. The locomotive came around the corner, and by the time the engine crew realized what had happened to the bridge, it was too late. At approximately 9:15 p.m., all but two of the passenger cars crashed into the stream and piled on top of each other. (Both, Fort Caspar Museum.)

The high waters and crushed cars made rescue efforts for survivors extremely difficult. While there are conflicting reports, it does appear that someone from the wreck walked over a mile to the nearest telephone to call for help. The rescue train arrived around 11:00 p.m., its headlights illuminating a grisly scene of twisted metal. Above, the remnants of the bridge at right show the drop the train made into the stream. Cleanup and recovery operations took several days. The Pullman car jutting into the air has become the most recognizable image of this wreck. Below, a steam-powered wrecking crane is lifting the car off the demolished express car underneath it. Amazingly, one of the coaches was completely rebuilt and placed back into service. (Both, Fort Caspar Museum.)

Prior to departure from Casper, engineer Ed Sprangler took control of the locomotive Colorado & Southern No. 350 and reviewed his orders with the conductor. He also received notice to use utmost caution due to the extreme weather, although the line had been inspected. The locomotive departed, pulling seven passenger cars including a mail car, express car, coaches, and Pullman sleepers. Rounding a corner before the bridge at Cole Creek, the headlight did not show the fact that the bridge had washed out until it was too late. Sprangler "dumped the air," a railroading term for making an emergency brake application, but the weight of the train and the wet rails left no chance for the train to stop before plummeting into the creek. (Natrona County Public Library Collection, CCWHC.)

Remainder of Locomotive after C.B.&Q. wreck. ColeCreek near Casper, Wyo. Sept. 27-1923

- Deluxe -

Plunging nose first into Cole Creek, the locomotive became buried deep in the streambed underneath the passenger cars. While extensive search efforts were made, engineer Sprangler's remains were not discovered until nearly two years later when a crew was working on the bridge. As one of the last large pieces of the train recovered, the locomotive appeared to have suffered catastrophic damage—indeed, there was little on the locomotive that escaped without becoming hopelessly bent, cracked, or broken. It was moved to the shops in Casper for evaluation, where it was determined that it could be repaired. The skeletal hulk was taken to the shops in Denver, where the locomotive was completely rebuilt and placed back on the Casper run. The rebuilt locomotive went on to serve another 27 years before being retired in 1950 and finally scrapped. (Natrona County Public Library Collection, CCWHC.)

Sixty-six passengers were on board the train when it departed Casper. Due to the hour of departure, many settled into their Pullman berths for the overnight ride. Despite the weather, the trip started out routinely, and the passengers had no concerns. Their first indication of a problem would have been a jolt as the brakes were hastily applied, followed by confusion and darkness as the cars left the tracks. Those passengers in the last two cars were fortunate, and injuries here were very minor. The train crew and passengers in those cars quickly became the first rescuers, attempting to reach survivors in the wrecked cars in the dark. The crushed nature of the cars, combined with the odd angles, made escape extremely difficult for those trapped inside. The survivors from the rear of the train did their best to reach survivors of the cars in Cole Creek by using the bell cords from the cars to create a guide rope. They entered the submerged cars several times in pitch-black conditions assisting others out. (Fort Caspar Museum.)

Of the 66 passengers aboard, the reported death toll was 31, though this number is in dispute. As bad as the wreck was, many passengers ticketed to be on the train delayed leaving Casper due to the weather, and the passenger load was the lightest it had been in the weeks leading up to the disaster. Wounded survivors were transported by the rescue train to Casper. Recovery of remains took months, as the floodwaters had carried some victims far downstream into the North Platte River. These photographs show the extent of the damage to the passenger cars. Above, a pile driver is beginning construction on a replacement bridge. (Above, CCWHC; below, Natrona County Public Library Collection, CCWHC.)

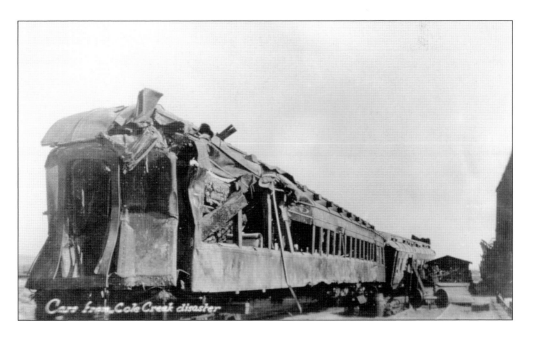

While disasters on the scale of the Cole Creek train wreck were the exception in central Wyoming railroading, other accidents did occur. These images show a wreck that happened somewhere near Casper. CB&Q locomotive No. 200 has completely left the tracks, along with a tank car to the right. Behind the tank car is another unidentified locomotive. One of the primary concerns with any wrecks involving freight trains leaving Casper would be oil spilled from the tank cars. Primary causes of wrecks in the early 1900s included damaged track, failure to follow train orders, fatigue of the crew, or mechanical problems. Railroading has always been hard, dangerous work, and small mistakes could, and often did, lead to severe consequences. (Thompson Collection, CCWHC.)

Due to the heavy tonnages and extreme forces involved, train wrecks can be catastrophic affairs. The steel rails that make up the track are nearly unrecognizable underneath CB&Q No. 200, though this engine has managed to remain upright. A cutting torch can be seen at lower right, soon to be used in cleanup efforts. For every hour that the line was closed, the railroad faced lost revenue. Therefore, the railroad would very quickly respond to any wreck with a wrecking train. These trains would have cranes, blocking, and space for a crew, often including bunk and kitchen cars. The crew would quickly and efficiently clear the line of the wreckage, while a track crew would repair track and reopen the line as soon as possible. If needed, temporary track would be laid to get delayed trains through, and then more time could be taken for a permanent fix. (Thompson Collection, CCWHC.)

Derailments and wrecks are not confined to the steam era. Pictured here is a Burlington Northern freight train derailment on June 15, 1985, along the West Yellowstone Highway in Casper. Above, the leading locomotive is still on the tracks; the one behind it derailed, but is still upright. Behind that, freight cars have completely turned over on their sides. Below, a diesel locomotive has been sent from the yard to couple on and pull away those cars at the rear of the train that were still on the track. (Both, Casper Star-Tribune Collection, CCWHC.)

This derailment occurred after railroad cars in the bentonite plant rolled down the siding and into the rest of the train as it passed, knocking those cars down the embankment. The open-topped hoppers were empty, saving a bigger mess that would have needed to be cleaned up. The vehicle at far right is a Burlington Northern crane preparing to start cleanup of the wrecked cars. On the left above, buildings and tanks of the Standard Oil Refinery are visible across the river. (Both, Casper Star-Tribune Collection, CCWHC.)

Another derailment occurred in June 1985 at Sodium, near the town of Natrona. The train had been traveling at 50 miles per hour when a broken wheel on a flatcar caused it to derail, spilling cargo, including an entire car of potatoes, along the track. Wrecks like this resulted not only in ruined equipment and damaged track but also insurance claims by those whose products were on the train. Numerous other wrecks and mishaps have happened over the years, though most were not as dramatic as those in this chapter. (Above, Casper Star-Tribune Collection, CCWHC; below, Charles Eckerson.)

Four

OIL DEFINES A CITY

With its discovery in the Salt Creek Field, oil was set to become an important component of the growing town of Casper, although the extent of its importance was underestimated. This 1925 view of tanks at the Standard Oil Refinery hints at the scale of the industry. (Fort Caspar Museum.)

Located between Center and Wolcott Streets, the Pennsylvania Oil & Gas refinery was the first to be built in Casper. Opening in 1895, the refinery processed 100 barrels of oil per day, producing 15 different types of lubricants for various types of machines. The refinery was closed in 1906. This photograph was taken looking southwest with Casper Mountain in the background. (Fort Caspar Museum.)

While the Standard Oil Refinery would grow to be the largest in the nation, it started with fairly humble origins. Here is a c. 1910s view of the Standard Manufacturing Plant, later called the Standard Oil Refinery. In addition to the large building, the surrounding tanks, piping, and smokestacks are all part of the plant. One lonely tank car is spotted outside the building, and a railroad crane is farther down the track. (Thompson Collection, CCWHC.)

During the height of oil production in Casper, long strings of tank cars would roll into and out of the town. From 1910 to 1924, the population grew from 2,639 to 32,276 people in the start of the continual boom-and-bust cycle that the city has become known for. It was declared that the town shipped more oil by rail than any other city in the world. (Fort Caspar Museum.)

The construction of the Standard Oil Refinery was a massive undertaking. Above, a steam-powered crane with a bucket for cement is seen along with a handful of workers. Below are the completed walls that supported the massive tanks. A boxcar sits on the tracks between the long lines of tanks used in the refining process. (Above, Thompson Collection, CCWHC; below, Fort Caspar Museum.)

This 1922 photograph shows tracks winding through the plant. Cars full of material for the plant as well as tank cars loaded with the refined product had to be moved into and out of the refinery 24 hours a day. (Natrona County Library Collection, CCWHC.)

The Standard Oil Refinery became one of the largest oil refineries in the world and as such was nearly impossible to photograph in a single frame. Even this aerial view, while capturing the majority of the plant, fails to include the outlying areas. Behind the refinery, long lines of tank cars are waiting to be loaded with finished products. (Blackmore Collection, CCWHC.)

In another view of the Standard Oil Refinery looking to the east, numerous storage tanks make up a large tank farm, and yard tracks are to the left. In 1922, more than one million barrels of crude oil were processed into gasoline and kerosene at this one refinery alone. (Blackmore Collection, CCWHC.)

The Standard Oil Refinery stands across the river, while in the foreground, work is underway on a project along the north bank of the North Platte River. Construction of the Standard Oil Refinery was completed in 1914, though it went through many changes over its long history. At its peak, it was one of the largest employers in central Wyoming. (David Historical Collection, CCWHC.)

While the Salt Creek Oil Field skyline was dominated by a forest of wooden oil derricks, a forest of chimneys at the refinery dominated the Casper skyline for 77 years. The refinery closed in 1991, and cleanup operations commenced, with the demolition of the complex being nearly absolute. Mitigation of the site took several years and millions of dollars. (McCleary family.)

BIRD'S EYE VIEW, CASPER, WYO, STANDARD REFINERY IN BACK-GROUND (DOUBLEDAY)

Residential and industrial areas of Casper were almost one and the same. Early Casper residents, many of whom lived in company housing, often became front-row spectators to accidents and mishaps at the refineries. Of primary concern were explosions at the refinery or the nitroglycerin storage bunkers for the oil fields, or derailments of the oil trains. One of the most spectacular oil-related disasters involved the large tank farms after lightning strikes caused the tanks to catch fire. The largest of these fires, below, spread to seven tanks, burning 500,000 barrels of oil on June 17 and 18, 1921. (Above, David Historical Collection, CCWHC; below, Western History Collection, CCWHC.)

In addition to the Standard Oil Refinery, there were several other refineries, large and small, in the Casper area. One of the largest early refineries, the Midwest Refinery, is seen in this photograph from 1913. The company owned many properties in the Salt Creek Oil Field and built pipelines to transfer oil to this refinery near present-day Mills. (Fort Caspar Museum.)

It was once a common sight to see trains leaving Casper composed of long strings of tank cars. A CB&Q locomotive pulls 39 tank cars loaded with high-quality lubricating oil from the Midwest Refining Company, visible to the left of the train. Wyoming's oil industry was one of the most vital national resources during wartime production for both of the world wars. (Natrona County Public Library Collection, CCWHC.)

On top of the noise of the refinery, Casper residents had to contend with the sound of riveting at the Union Tank Lines shop 24 hours a day as tank cars were repaired. To move these cars through the refinery, the Standard Oil Company owned switch locomotives. One such switch locomotive, a small 0-4-0 tank locomotive, can be visited today at the Colorado Railroad Museum in Golden, Colorado. (Fort Caspar Museum.)

A train of tank cars, with passenger cars at the back, travels along the North Platte River. Crude oil was moved from the Salt Creek Oil Field to Casper behind horse-drawn wagons in the early days and later by pipeline. Refined products, including kerosene, gasoline, and lubricants, were then shipped by rail all over the United States and exported overseas. (David Historical Collection, CCWHC.)

Commencing operations in 1923, the North South Railroad was a 41-mile short line railroad that connected with the CB&Q near Casper. Known as the "Oil Fields Line" or the "Up and Down Line" locally, the railroad transported passengers, supplies, and oil in and out of the Salt Creek Oil Field. The railroad could not compete with the pipelines and ceased operations in 1935. (Garrett Collection, CCWHC.)

The wooden derricks of the Salt Creek Oil Field became a lasting symbol of the oil industry in Wyoming. A reconstruction of a derrick stands today in Casper at the corner of Poplar Street and the West Yellowstone Highway. (Chuck Morrison Collection, CCWHC.)

In an example of early photo doctoring, this promotional panorama was created from the photograph on page 69. The sign indicates that the train was carrying lubricating oil from the Midwest Refining Company for export to Europe. For whatever reason, the refinery itself was removed

from the original photograph. Looking closely at the image, one can see the "corrected" tank cars after the removal of signs and telephone poles seen in the original. (Fort Caspar Museum.)

THE MIDWEST REFINING CO.
Trainload Shipment
LUBRICATING OIL
Bright Filtered Cylinder Stock
FOR EXPORT TO EUROPE

Casper's oil refineries, after being such a large part of the city's history, have now all but vanished. The Standard Oil Refinery was renamed Amoco in 1985 and closed in 1991. Here, modern tank cars are loaded at the plant prior to its closure. Today, the Sinclair Oil Refinery is the Casper area's only remaining refinery. However, oil and gas development still remains an important part of the local economy. (Both, Fort Caspar Museum.)

Five

COMMUNITIES TIED BY STEEL

The arrival of the rails provided strong connections between all the communities along the line. Express parcel shipments were picked up either at a depot or the express company's building nearby and were typically carried in the express compartment of a passenger train. Pictured here is the American Express Company building in Glenrock, located near the depot. (Wyoming State Archives.)

Central Wyoming agriculture was dominated by the wool industry in the early 1900s. The first stop on the C&NW line west of Casper was called Cadoma. Marvin Bishop, who had been ranching in the area since 1898, owned and operated large shearing pens there. Numerous ranches brought their sheep to these pens to be sheared, and the wool was then loaded directly into boxcars for shipment to market. Ramps were also located here to load sheep into stockcars. A nearby stop on the CB&Q line had additional pens and was named Bishop. The photograph shows a group posed in Cadoma next to a siding coming off of the main line. Note the sign for the stop lying on a post on the ground. (Cadoma Foundation.)

Early residents of central Wyoming experienced a long, rough trip over rough roads and trails by wagon or horseback. Many men who had come ahead to start a homestead found that their wives were less than impressed with the journey to their new home. Once here, they found that few aside from the closest neighbors were willing to make the trek for a visit. The railroad changed all of this, providing comfortable transportation to these small communities. Now family and friends could make trips to visit for pleasure or for business. Traveling salesmen could also be found visiting the small towns along the track, bringing the latest modern conveniences to rural Wyoming. Here, a woman is pictured with her baggage in Natrona, 30 miles west of Casper. (Hutchison Collection, CCWHC.)

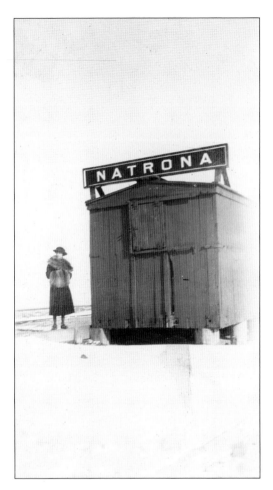

The same woman from the previous page is pictured at left next to the C&NW "depot" at Natrona, while below, a family has dressed in their best to greet her. The depot was an old wooden boxcar set off the tracks on blocks. Such structures were commonly placed at stops that did not warrant the cost of a dedicated building, or were used as temporary structures until a more permanent depot could be built. Many such cars can still be found scattered throughout the West after they were sold to individuals for use as sheds. (Both, Hutchison Collection, CCWHC.)

It was a chilly winter day as a C&NW passenger train with a steam locomotive pulling three passenger cars paused next to the Natrona station. Such stops were often referred to as "whistle stop" or "flag stop" stations, meaning that the train did not actually stop unless requested by a passenger on the train or flagged down by a passenger at the station. Without a station agent at the stop, the passengers would board the train, and the conductor would sell them a ticket for the ride. The telegraph lines along the tracks were used by the railroad's dispatchers to relay train orders along the line in the days before radio communication. The town of Natrona was never a large community, although a post office, opened in 1906, lasted until 1984. (Hutchison Collection, CCWHC.)

The center of social life in Natrona was the general store. For such a small community, the store had two very important amenities in addition to goods. First was the gas pump to the right above. A sign propped up next to the barrels advertises Texaco gasoline, which was most likely delivered by train along with most of the goods for sale inside. The second amenity offered was a telephone booth provided by the Bell Telephone Company. A variety of canned goods line the shelves behind the children in the photograph below. (Both, Hutchison Collection, CCWHC.)

Affectionately called Natrona's "streetcar" in the family album these photographs came from, the vehicle being posed on is actually a track inspection cart used by a section man. The railroad was divided into sections, with men assigned to inspect and conduct light repairs of the track. The earliest inspection carts were powered by hand and came in the form of a velocipede, similar to a rail-bike, or a handcar. This small cart was a giant leap forward from those, as there was a gas motor that propelled the cart along the tracks. (Both, Hutchison Collection, CCWHC.)

Typical of many small, rural Wyoming communities, the town of Natrona did not boast much in the way of services. While some communities did survive and still have a small population today, most have faded away. With the development of good roads and the rise of the automobile, ranchers and others who lived near such towns found it easier to travel to the larger towns for their supplies, social events, and education for their children rather than using the trains. Pictured here is a homestead near the town of Natrona. (Hutchison Collection, CCWHC.)

The town of Powder River, 38 miles west of Casper, was one of the larger stops between Casper and Shoshoni. The post office was opened in 1904, and a modest depot was constructed by the C&NW in 1910. The depot survived and was listed in the National Register of Historic Places in 1988. (Casper Star-Tribune Collection, CCWHC.)

Located 48 miles west of Casper, the town of Waltman warranted a modest depot building. After passenger service ended on a line, it was not uncommon for railroads to retain the depot buildings in such remote locations, where they were converted to housing for maintenance workers. (Chuck Morrison Collection, CCWHC.)

Arminto, 60 miles west of Casper, was another speck on the map reached in 1913 by the CB&Q as construction progressed to Casper. Another stop that did not warrant a full station, a small telephone shack was constructed next to the track. To the right of the main track is a track inspection vehicle called a "speeder." (Casper Star-Tribune Collection, CCWHC.)

Lacking a dining car for passengers to have a meal on board, this C&NW train stopped at Moneta, 77 miles from Casper, for passengers to step off the train to eat around 1907. The train would pause while passengers disembarked, enjoyed a hearty meal, and then reboarded to continue their trip, though the stop could be cut short if the train was late. (Cutshaw Collection, CCWHC.)

As they had for all the other towns along the line, large crowds turned out to greet the first train into the town of Lander in 1906. Onlookers crowded along the tracks, with those who could not get a good view climbing on top of boxcars on the adjacent tracks. Many of those who came out for the festivities dressed in their finest clothes. It was very common for celebrations like these to spread beyond the railroad depot. Bands would play, families would picnic, banquets would be prepared, dances were held, speeches were made, and stores hosted special sales. The passengers had plenty of time to take in the excitement as the train was prepared for the return trip to Casper. (Both, Cutshaw Collection, CCWHC.)

With not enough passengers to cover the expenses of a full passenger train from Casper to Lander, the C&NW looked for another solution to cut operating expenses. The solution was a self-propelled railcar affectionately called a "Doodlebug." Pictured during a station stop in Riverton, the engineer is standing in the door to the cab, followed by a small Railway Post Office compartment complete with a mail hook, a baggage compartment, and finally a section of coach seating for the passengers. (Cutshaw Collection, CCWHC.)

It had been many years since the last passenger had passed through the Lander depot when this photograph was taken in November 1972. C&NW locomotive No. 710 is on the point of the last train to leave town. After 66 years of service, the rails would be pulled up, though the depot building would survive, serving many years as the location of the chamber of commerce (Cutshaw Collection, CCWHC.)

The town of Riverton was founded in 1906 in anticipation of the railroad's arrival and the opening of the Wind River Reservation. Seen here, C&NW diesel locomotive No. 4136 is at the Riverton depot. Like the depot in Lander, the Riverton depot would survive the end of the C&NW and be repurposed. (Cutshaw Collection, CCWHC.)

With walls towering 2,500 feet above the canyon bottom, the Wind River Canyon between Shoshoni and Thermopolis has been a scenic highlight for travelers since the first rails were laid through it in 1911. The CB&Q built south through the canyon and encountered numerous engineering challenges placing the rails along the river, including the boring of several tunnels. The image at left was captured from a passenger train around 1940. Below, passengers have stepped off a train to pose for a group photograph. A camera has been set up at lower right. (Left, Fort Caspar Museum; below, Wyoming State Archives.)

Tracks through the Wind River Canyon were laid down on the west side of the river between 1910 and 1911, fourteen years before the road on the east side was constructed. In May 1911, the first train south through the canyon reached the new terminus at Boysen. It was another two years before construction continued toward Casper and eventually east to Orin Junction. Work did not end with the completion of the line; rockslides became common occurrences, an issue that still plagues modern-day railroad operations. Routine inspection of the line is done to ensure that trains can pass through safely. Here, detector cars use equipment to find any invisible flaws in the track in August 1967. (Charles Eckerson.)

Burlington Depot, Thermopolis, Wyo.

CB&Q tracks reached Thermopolis from Greybull in May 1910, with the first train arriving on June 24. With the help of the railroad line, Thermopolis became a popular tourist destination, with people traveling from far away to visit the world's largest mineral hot springs and ride through the spectacular scenery of the Wind River Canyon. Above, a large number of passengers wait to board the train in the 1920s after their visit. Below is how the depot appeared in the 1960s. (Above, David Historical Collection, CCWHC; below, Charles Eckerson.)

In the days before highways and airliners, passenger trains were the primary connection between communities. One could board a train in a small town like Powder River and travel anywhere in the country in speed and comfort, well taken care of by attentive and friendly train crews. The end of widespread passenger service fundamentally changed the way Americans traveled and in a sense was the end of an American institution. Today, rail passengers only see a pale imitation of what was American passenger railroading. (Both, Thompson Collection, CCWHC.)

Dressed more like a cowboy than a railroader, the worker above loads sacks of mail into the Railway Post Office car during the train's station stop in Lovell in 1967. Farther down the platform, another worker is loading baggage and shipments into the baggage car. In a rare view below, the inside of the baggage car is seen. In addition to passengers' checked baggage, express parcels were often carried in these cars, along with fresh milk in cans, as seen at lower left. (Both, Charles Eckerson.)

Six

SPECIAL TRAINS

Many railroads maintain a fleet of passenger cars that can be used for a variety of official business functions. C&NW No. 402, an EMD F7 preserved by the railroad to pull these trains, brought this special train through Casper for a cross-country tour on October 27, 1982. The locomotive was retired in 1996 and sold to the Royal Gorge Route Railroad in Colorado, where it still pulls excursion trains today. (Casper Star-Tribune Collection, CCWHC.)

Railroads have often been called on to carry oversized cargo. In this case, a large vessel resting on two flatcars moves over the C&NW through Casper. Casper photographer Thomas Carrigen stopped and shot these two images while the train paused outside the Casper depot on October 1, 1932. The short consist was made up of 4-6-0 steam locomotive No. 375, two flatcars, caboose No. 2160, and officer's car No. 404. Heavy moves such as this required careful planning to ensure that the train could cross any bridges and fit through close-clearance areas like cuts and tunnels so that no damage was done to the cargo or the rail line. (Both, Wyoming State Archives.)

CB&Q officer's car No. 100 is pictured in the Burlington yards near the Casper depot. This was part of the fleet of such cars that the railroad had for use by company executives and their guests while on inspection trips. The car included a kitchen, dining room, office, bedrooms, and observation lounge. This photograph was taken sometime after 1951. A wooden caboose is also in the yard and can be seen in the background on the right. Today, special inspection trains still occasionally pass through central Wyoming. (Casper Star-Tribune Collection, CCWHC.)

Ten years after the last steam locomotive pulled a regular train out of Casper, CB&Q No. 4960 was scheduled to make a visit to celebrate the 50th anniversary of that railroad arriving in town. In honor of the occasion, the locomotive was painted gold and drew large crowds of local citizens. The locomotive had been saved by the CB&Q after steam service on the line officially ended, was given a full overhaul, and entered service as an excursion locomotive touring the entire CB&Q system. Excursion service was cancelled after 1966, and the locomotive was sold to the Circus World Museum. Since then, it has jumped to various museums and railroads. Today, it serves on the Grand Canyon Railway, where it once again pulls excursions. (Above, CCWHC; below, Charles Eckerson.)

The steam locomotives that ran out of Casper used fuel oil in their fireboxes. No. 4960 was a coal-burning locomotive, so when it visited, a way was needed to load coal into the tender. The solution was to use a diesel-powered crane with a clamshell bucket, shown above, to load the tender one scoop at a time in an effective but time-consuming process. The crew assigned to it took every opportunity to inspect the locomotive, seen below, to ensure that all the moving parts were well lubricated. (Both, Charles Eckerson.)

No. 4960's visit to central Wyoming did not get off to a good start. On the way to Casper, the engineer assigned to the locomotive, who was well known to be a fast runner, was attempting to raise smoke through Douglas and came into the town at 40 miles per hour. Ahead was train No. 29 stopped at the depot. No. 4960 was unable to come to a stop before colliding with the rear of the passenger train, pushing that train forward and breaking the pilot beam and flattening the headlight on the locomotive. When it was brought to the shops in Casper, Charles Eckerson, posing in both photographs, volunteered to help make repairs. While shop crews got to work, the master mechanic drove to Lincoln, Nebraska, to get a replacement headlight off the scrap line. (Both, Charles Eckerson.)

Among the more exotic visitors to Casper was Queen Marie of Romania. The queen arrived in the United States in October 1926 and embarked on a tour of North America, being received by massive crowds everywhere she visited. Here, the queen (in furs) has just stepped off the royal train at the Burlington Depot accompanied by Gov. Nellie Tayloe Ross and surrounded by a large crowd eager to catch a glimpse of royalty. As a parting memento, Queen Marie presented Natrona County High School with a signed football that remained on display for many years, though its whereabouts are currently unknown. (Both, David Memorial Collection, CCWHC.)

Railroads across the country strove to find ways to bring revenue to their companies and revitalize passenger service during the Great Depression. Decreased passenger numbers meant that revenue on many trains could not cover the operational costs of the heavy passenger cars and steam locomotives. The CB&Q responded by developing a lightweight, articulated passenger train. This articulated train set, originally named the Burlington Zephyr, while not the first internal-combustion-powered streamliner, held the distinction of being the first diesel-powered streamliner in the United States. The three-car set had a Railway Post Office compartment, baggage and express space, a buffet-kitchen, coach seating, and an observation compartment. Eventually renamed the Pioneer Zephyr, it was made famous by a record-breaking trip between Denver and Chicago. The train was displayed at the Burlington Depot in Casper in 1934 while on a nationwide tour. It has been preserved and can be toured at the Chicago Museum of Science and Industry. (Wyoming State Archives.)

Publicity stunts have long been used by companies to promote products or services, so the CB&Q pulled out all the stops to snag headlines across the country. After months of preparations and testing, it was announced that the Pioneer Zephyr was set to make a dawn-to-dusk trip from Denver, Colorado, to Chicago, Illinois, on May 26, 1934. The CB&Q ensured that nothing would stop the train by spiking the switches, diverting every other train to side tracks, and posting police at every road crossing. Thirteen hours and five minutes after leaving Denver, the Pioneer Zephyr arrived in Chicago, one hour and 55 minutes ahead of schedule. The run was made nonstop, with the train reaching a top speed of 112 miles per hour and an average speed of 77 miles per hour. It was then put on display at the Century of Progress Fair before making a systemwide tour to over 200 cities in 31 states. The nation was captivated by the story, as evidenced by the large crowd that turned out in Casper. (Wyoming State Archives.)

The arrival of Pres. Harry S. Truman in May 1950 meant that the Burlington yard in Casper needed to look its best. The depot was decked out with oversized bunting, and crowds were kept back on the east side of the building. Much like today, moving the president was no small task. The presidential train not only had space for the president in the last car, it also carried a communications car, a hospital car, and numerous cars for advisors, staffers, reporters, and other dignitaries. Carrying such an important passenger, the train moved under a code name and took top priority over all other trains. While an effort was made to make the train appear normal, the security along the line wherever it traveled soon gave away its identity. (Chuck Morrison Collection, CCWHC.)

It was very rare for the president to come to town, and as such, it caused quite a stir. Large crowds turned out to the Burlington yards to hear the president's speech and get a chance to see him up close. Bands played, and every effort was made to put forth the true Western hospitality that Casper has always been known for. Here, railroad workers have taken a break from their duties to hear President Truman's speech. Behind them, a soldier and more crowds are on the Center Street overpass. (Chuck Morrison Collection, CCWHC.)

Due to security concerns brought about by World War II, it was determined that the president needed a dedicated railcar that would ensure his safety. Thus, the *Ferdinand Magellan* was pulled from the Pullman private car pool and specially outfitted with armor plating and bulletproof windows. Weighing 285,000 pounds, this was the heaviest passenger car in the nation. The car traveled all across the United States and was utilized by three presidents on official government business; one also used it on a special campaign trip. Hundreds of speeches were given from the rear platform of the car through special loudspeakers permanently attached over the observation platform. Here, President Truman gives a speech from the back of the car at the Burlington Depot on May 8, 1950. Truman had come to Casper to visit the Kortes Dam project west of town. Today, this car can be found at the Gold Coast Railroad Museum in Miami, Florida. (Chuck Morrison Collection, CCWHC.)

As part of the welcome for President Truman, the Casper Band performed. Above, Truman poses with band members while surrounded by reporters, aides, and security officers. At right, accompanying the president were Neal Forsling (left), a prominent Wyoming artist, and Bess Truman, photographed in the vestibule of one of the cars enjoying the warm welcome. (Both, Chuck Morrison Collection, CCWHC.)

Pres. Theodore Roosevelt was well known for his dedication to conservation, and made several visits to the Cowboy State. A highly popular president, his travels through the state saw him on long horseback tours, hunting expeditions in the mountains, and observing the Cheyenne Frontier Days rodeo. Gov. Bryant B. Brooks, the only governor of the state to come from Casper, hosted the president at the governor's mansion in Cheyenne and developed a strong working relationship that translated into many Wyoming monuments and parks. On one such visit, the president arrived in Casper by train and spoke to large crowds from a special presidential box at the C&NW station, one of the hundreds of speeches he would give in Wyoming. It is surmised that this special box traveled with the president, as it can also be seen in photographs taken in Cheyenne. (Frances Seely Webb Collection, CCWHC.)

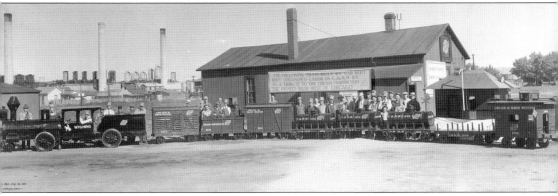

The C&NW was a big part of a parade on August 30, 1936. The highlight was a replica, not shown, of the first steam locomotive that came to the plains on the C&NW line. It was built by railroad employees in Chicago as a faithful reproduction and was featured in parades in towns along the CB&Q route. In addition, the railroad entered various wagons, automobiles, and hand cars to follow behind the model. The shop employees from Casper donated personal time to build this miniature train to be part of the spectacle. All of this combined to make a highly memorable parade entry for Casper youth. (Western History Collection, CCWHC.)

An elephant exits from its special train car on the Ringling Brothers and Barnum & Bailey Circus train on August 22, 1985, in the CB&Q yard in Casper. The elephant would soon be a part of one of the most anticipated circus traditions, the animal walk from the railroad siding to the site of the show. The line of animals and performers made their way through downtown and up the path to the Casper Events Center. These processions would traditionally feature brightly colored wagons, music, clowns, performers, and animals and would create excitement for the upcoming spectacle, ensuring that no one could miss the fact that "The Greatest Show on Earth" was in town. (Casper Star-Tribune Collection, CCWHC.)

In the early days of the circus, the animals were used to pull the colorful wagons loaded with everything the show needed, but by the time these photographs were taken, the animal walk was more of a publicity parade to build up excitement, as the show had moved into stadium buildings. These photographs show the animal walk on August 22, 1985, which left the CB&Q railyards going through downtown before working its way to Poplar Street and up the bike path to the Casper Events Center for the big show. The menagerie included llamas, horses, camels, zebras, and elephants. As part of the parade, Casper's mayor, Mary Behrens, rode one of the elephants. (Both, Casper Star-Tribune Collection, CCWHC.)

After the performances, the performers and animals made their way back to the Burlington yards to board the train and leave town on August 25, 1985. The train departed Casper for its next show in Billings, Montana. The train was making good time until it derailed in the town of Lovell, Wyoming. Most of the cars came off the track, but all remained upright, and there were no serious injuries. (Both, Casper Star-Tribune Collection, CCWHC.)

Many Lovell residents turned out for the "Greatest Show in Lovell," which consisted of railroad crews with cranes carefully placing each of the derailed cars back on the track. While the Burlington Northern returned the cars to the tracks, the circus had a full mechanical crew on the train with their own shop, store of parts, and tools to inspect and repair any problems found with the circus cars. Apparently the circus train suffered little damage from the incident, and it soon departed north into Montana. Here, two local residents observe as car No. 89 is rerailed. (Casper Star-Tribune Collection, CCWHC.)

The first P.T. Barnum Circus train left Columbus, Ohio, in 1872, starting a tradition that would last 145 years. Barnum's circus continued to grow and was eventually combined with Ringling Brothers. From the first humble 60-car train came the greatest circus train in the world—twice that length and consisting of passenger, livestock, and freight cars. In the last year of operation, 2017, the Ringling Brothers and Barnum & Bailey Circus train was the longest privately owned train in the world. When the circus train made its last run, it ended one of the most colorful aspects of railroading history. Pictured here, the elephants have been loaded back into their cars and are ready to depart Casper in 1985. (Casper Star-Tribune Collection, CCWHC.)

Seven

INTO THE MODERN ERA

The Amoco Refinery, as the Standard Oil Refinery was named after 1985, was one of the most recognizable features of Casper. After nearly 90 years of operation, the last barrel of oil was refined on December 13, 1991, and the refinery was closed. Demolition of the refinery and subsequent cleanup was no small task. Today, the site is the location of the Three Crowns Golf Course. (Chuck Morrison Collection, CCWHC.)

Every train entering or leaving the Casper railyard to the east crosses the steel bridge over Interstate 25. Any damage to this bridge by oversized loads brings all rail operations to a standstill. Here, workers inspect and repair the underside of the bridge after a truck collided with it. Repairs were completed in short order, and rail operations were soon resumed. (Casper Star-Tribune Collection, CCWHC.)

Looking east on First Street, Burlington Northern employee Dwight Golder is seen on the bridge of the crossing lights on May 16, 1989. There were tracks branching off from the Casper railyard that accessed the industrial buildings of the Old Yellowstone District. (Casper Star-Tribune Collection, CCWHC.)

Traffic on Durbin Street in Casper was temporarily disrupted while C&NW maintenance crews completed some repairs to the track through the crossing on June 22, 1987. To the right of the work is the sign for the First Wyoming Bank. Less than 10 years later, the tracks would be gone after the C&NW merged with the Union Pacific Railroad and it was announced that the line would be abandoned between Casper and Orin Junction. Today, the former line has been preserved in a sense as a bicycle trail cutting through town. (Casper Star-Tribune Collection, CCWHC.)

The last passenger train left the C&NW Depot on August 10, 1950, though the building lasted until demolition commenced in July 1988. Far from being knocked over quickly with a bulldozer, workers slowly dismantled the building. Above, a final view of the front of the depot was captured right before demolition began. Below, workers are removing the roof over the baggage portion of the building, while other workers have knocked out the end wall. The Pioneer Monument was moved to a park on Center Street across from the county courthouse. Today, the site of the old depot is a parking lot with little indication that this spot was once the center of life in the city. (Both, Casper Star-Tribune Collection, CCWHC.)

The Burlington Depot still stands as an imposing structure at the end of Wolcott Street. After service as a passenger depot, the Trailways Bus Company used it as a bus depot from the 1960s to the 1980s. Today, the building retains much of its original appearance. The Burlington Railroad Station sign remains above the second-floor windows, although the CB&Q logo and bus depot signs have been removed. The biggest change from the building's historic appearance was the removal of the cage on the right side. The BNSF Railway still uses the building for modern railway operations. (Casper Star-Tribune Collection, CCWHC.)

Walnut Street was blocked for an entire day on January 30, 1988, after a locomotive and eight empty tank cars derailed. Here, two workers jack up one of the empty tank cars, which weighed approximately 35 tons. (Casper Star-Tribune Collection, CCWHC.)

After it was damaged by a derailment, the Burlington Northern replaced a section of track and left behind the old wooden ties along the West Yellowstone Highway. Here, Chuck Calkinn (left) and Wade Ravert collect the old ties on June 23, 1987. They were sold by a local company for $4 to $8 apiece for landscaping and other uses and could be found all over Casper. (Casper Star-Tribune Collection, CCWHC.)

In 1979, the Burlington Northern launched construction on what was considered the longest stretch of new railroad built in the United States since 1931. It connected the line at Orin north to the town of Gillette through the rich Powder River Basin coalfields. A far cry from the manual work of laying track at the start of the century, workers utilized the most modern devices to lay track quickly and efficiently. Here, a machine drives the spikes that hold the rails to the crossties. Below, the spiked and ballasted track is ready for service. (Both, Casper Star-Tribune Collection, CCWHC.)

The 116-mile stretch of new track took 3,100 ties for every mile. Above, the ties are laid down and made ready for tie plates and rails. Below, a car loaded with ties waits while, on the next track over, a long string of ballast cars stretches down the new line. Ballast, typically consisting of crushed stone, ensures water drainage and provides structure for the track. The track was designed to handle 110-car coal trains hauling 11,000 tons of coal each from the mines in the Powder River Basin to powerplants all over the United States. (Both, Casper Star-Tribune Collection, CCWHC.)

In another break from early railroad construction, the Orin line was built using continuously welded rail. In the image above, the main line is the track on the left, while the ties with tie plates laid down are for a siding. The machine below is laying down quarter-mile lengths of rail onto the freshly laid ties. The ends of these sections would be welded together, creating one smooth route. This took away the traditional clickety-clack sound of the train's wheels over the jointed rail. While this removed some of the romance of the railroads, it created a smoother ride and eliminated some of the stress caused by trains rolling over the line. (Both, Casper Star-Tribune Collection, CCWHC.)

With the new Orin line completed, the Powder River Basin mines were set to meet the growing demands of the nation's industrial needs. When the line was opened in 1979, forty trains a day was considered busy. By the peak of coal production in the basin in 2008, there were over 100 trains every day coming into and leaving the coalfields. Called unit trains, they can be thought of as a conveyor belt. Here, they pass below the coal silos, where they can be loaded without needing to stop. The loaded train would travel to a powerplant, be unloaded, and return back to the basin for another load. (Both, Casper Star-Tribune Collection, CCWHC.)

At the peak of production in 2008, the mines of the Powder River Basin produced almost 500 million tons of coal, providing over half of the nation's energy needs. The Black Thunder Mine and the North Antelope/Rochelle Mines competed to be the largest surface coal mines in the world. Trains from the basin could be found delivering coal in over 30 different states. To make the entire process as efficient as possible, the train entered a loop of track to the coal silos, which turned the train and prepared it for the return journey to the powerplant while it was being loaded. The concrete silos were designed to load an entire train with 11,000 tons of coal, 100 tons in each car. (Casper Star-Tribune Collection, CCWHC.)

To honor their close connections with the communities along their lines, railroads across the country have donated old steam locomotives and other rolling stock to various towns and museums. In 1962, the CB&Q donated steam locomotive No. 5633 to the State of Wyoming, and it was put on display at the Wyoming State Fairgrounds in Douglas. The locomotive was later moved into a park at the old FE&MV Depot and donated to the City of Douglas. As the centerpiece of the Douglas Railroad Interpretive Center, it is surrounded by several passenger cars, including a coach, baggage car, sleeping car, and dining car, along with a livestock car, caboose, and a speeder. The restored depot is listed in the National Register of Historic Places. (McCleary family.)

Over 130 years have passed since rails first entered central Wyoming. In that time, the rails have brought sweeping changes to the region. While today most of central Wyoming's citizens barely give freight trains more than a passing glance, it must be remembered that at one time, the railroads formed the backbone of the region and were at the center of nearly every aspect of life. From immigrants to royalty, people came from all over the world, each leaving a mark on the combined cultural heritage of the region. Goods and materials brought the growth of industry, whose products were sent all over the United States. Today's railroading is a far cry from that of yesteryear, yet if one looks hard enough, remnants of the past remain. Even the caboose occasionally makes an appearance, though like many things, its primary function has changed. No longer does it house a train crew traveling between towns; now, it serves as a platform for train crews to ride during switching chores in town. (Casper Star-Tribune Collection, CCWHC.)

BIBLIOGRAPHY

Dodson, G.B. "Wyoming Tales and Trails." www.wyomingtalesandtrails.com.

King, Robert. *Trails to Rails: A History of Wyoming's Railroad.* Casper, WY: Mountain States Lithographing, 2005.

Kukura, Edna G., and Susan Niethammer True. *Casper: A Pictorial History.* Virginia Beach, VA: The Donning Company Publishers, 1986.

Randall, Art. *Casper "Old Town" and Fremont, Elkhorn and Missouri Valley Railroad.* Casper, WY: Mountain States Lithographing, 1989.

Wyoming State Historical Society. www.wyohistory.org.

ABOUT THE AUTHOR

Con Trumbull was born and raised on his family's ranch southeast of Casper. A fifth-generation Wyoming rancher, he has always had a love of the history of Wyoming and especially of the railroads. Trumbull graduated from Natrona County High School, attended Casper College, and eventually earned a bachelor of science degree in geology from Colorado Mesa University in Grand Junction, Colorado. He works at the Nevada Northern Railway as the archivist and is a steam locomotive fireman and engineer, diesel locomotive engineer, conductor, and train dispatcher. Trumbull has also been a longtime member of the Fort Caspar Museum Association both as a board member and a museum volunteer.

DISCOVER THOUSANDS OF LOCAL HISTORY BOOKS
FEATURING MILLIONS OF VINTAGE IMAGES

Arcadia Publishing, the leading local history publisher in the United States, is committed to making history accessible and meaningful through publishing books that celebrate and preserve the heritage of America's people and places.

Find more books like this at
www.arcadiapublishing.com

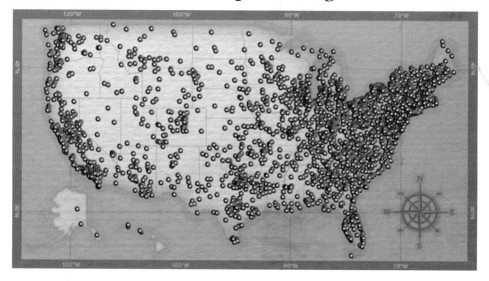

Search for your hometown history, your old stomping grounds, and even your favorite sports team.